# Teaching
# WARRIORS DON'T CRY

### Created to accompany
### the memoir by Melba Pattillo Beals

**FACING HISTORY & OURSELVES**

Facing History and Ourselves is an international educational and professional development organization whose mission is to challenge teachers and their students to stand up to bigotry and hate. For more information about Facing History and Ourselves, please visit our website at www.facinghistory.org.

Last updated January 2022.

ISBN: 978-1-940457-24-6

# CONTENTS

# USING THIS STUDY GUIDE

**Note on edition:** This study guide is based on *Warriors Don't Cry*, abridged edition, by Melba Pattillo Beals (Simon Pulse, 1995), ISBN: 978-1-4169-4882-7.

**Teaching strategies, videos, and media referenced throughout this guide can be found at facinghistory.org/warriors-media.**

In May of 1954, the United States Supreme Court ruled in *Brown v. Board of Education of Topeka, et al.,* that racial segregation in the nation's public schools is unconstitutional. *Warriors Don't Cry* is a first-person account of one attempt to turn that ruling into a social reality. Melba Pattillo Beals was one of nine African American students chosen to desegregate Central High School in Little Rock, Arkansas, in the fall of 1957. Her memoir chronicles the terror and fear—as well as the courage and determination—that marked her experiences and those of the other eight African American students who attended the high school that year.

This resource is designed to guide teachers and students through an experience of *Warriors Don't Cry* that engages the mind, heart, and conscience. This approach will develop students' literacy skills, promote their historical understanding of a key moment in the civil rights movement, deepen their understanding of racism, and foster empathy, perspective taking, and other social-emotional skills. Most importantly, the goal of this guide is to kindle in students a sense of civic agency, a belief that they can, alone or with others, make a positive difference in their school, community, or nation.

Note: For further background information and lessons on the Little Rock Nine and integration of Central High School, see Facing History's unit **Choices in Little Rock** at facinghistory.org/warriors-media.

## Exploring the Central Question

*Warriors Don't Cry* describes the choices Melba Pattillo Beals and other students made in Little Rock during the 1957–1958 school year. Beals's story helps to illuminate both the importance of confronting racism and the risks involved. The central question below is designed to help students connect their discussions and activities about Beals's particular story with this larger theme:

**Q:** *What can we do, alone and with others, to confront racism? How can we as individuals and as citizens make a positive difference in our school, community, and nation?*

The central question is introduced in Section 1: Defining Segregation and revisited regularly in subsequent sections. By returning to the central question at regular intervals, students will be able to trace how their thinking has developed and deepened over the course of their study of the memoir. The discussion questions and activities throughout this guide also support students' exploration of the central question, and the guide concludes with a suggested writing assignment based on this question.

## Section Elements

This resource is organized into six sections, each designed to support the careful reading of specific pages of the memoir. Each section is broken into three main components (and, in some cases, an optional fourth):

- **Exploring the Text:** primarily text-based questions designed to deepen students' understanding of the memoir and to prompt reflection on its themes. You can use these—and your own—questions as journal or discussion prompts to guide students' exploration of the text. The questions in this section are grouped to focus on particular themes or subthemes. As students respond to the questions, encourage them to refer to passages or examples from the book to support their ideas.

- **Connecting to the Central Question:** a repeating prompt for students to connect what they have learned from activities and analysis in each section to the larger theme of confronting racism and making a positive difference. By returning to the central question in each section of the memoir, students will be able to trace how their thinking has developed and deepened over the course of their study of *Warriors Don't Cry*.

- **Activities for Deeper Understanding:** suggestions for writing, reflection, and discussion-based activities that support literary analysis, provide historical context, and introduce additional perspectives on the events that take place in the memoir. When appropriate, these activities also invite students to make thematic connections between *Warriors Don't Cry* and other texts and universal human behaviors. Choose from these activities to find those that best suit your learning goals and the needs of your students.

- **Extension Activities:** suggestions for writing, reflection, and research that, while not essential to a study of the memoir, help students develop a deeper and broader understanding of the crisis in Little Rock in 1957, its historical context, and factors that influenced the choices people made.

Section 1 also includes a series of pre-reading activities designed to introduce key themes and concepts before students begin to read the memoir.

While it is crucial that students have the opportunity to respond to *Warriors Don't Cry* both intellectually and emotionally, the extent to which teachers engage their students in the activities in this guide that extend beyond the pages of the memoir itself will vary depending on available class time and the support students need in understanding the text.

## Helping Students Process Emotionally Powerful Material

*Warriors Don't Cry* captures Melba Pattillo Beals's personal experiences as she stood on the front lines of a civil rights battle in 1957. Many of the stories and images—as well as the insults and epithets expressed by protestors—are emotionally troubling and even graphic. The deeply personal and emotional events that Beals documents can help to foster engagement and empathy in students, yet they can also be disturbing.

Before you begin to teach the book, it's important to acknowledge that students may have a range of emotional reactions to this challenging text. Some students may respond with sadness, anger, or disgust, while others may not find the story powerful to the same degree. In addition, different people demonstrate emotion in different ways. Some students will be silent. Some may laugh. Some may not want to talk. Some may take days to process difficult stories.

## Establishing a Safe Space

The resources in this lesson probe themes related to race, racism, and history that feel deeply personal to many people. Therefore, it is important to begin the unit by preparing students to engage honestly, but civilly and respectfully, with these topics. The following activities are designed to create a safe space for dialogue throughout the unit:

1. Start with a journal prompt. Tell students that the following writing exercise is a *private* journal entry that they will not be asked to share with anyone, so they should feel free to write their most honest reflection. Have students take several minutes to complete this sentence: "I *mostly* feel _____ when discussing race, because _____."

2. Now that students have gathered their thoughts, tell them that you are going to do a group brainstorm. They should not make "I" statements or share how they feel or what they wrote. Tell students: Let's put words on the board that represent the feelings that we think may be in the room when we discuss race. At this point, we will just list and not comment on them.

3. Now look at the list. Ask students: What do the words have in common? *(Usually the words are mostly, but maybe not all, negative.)* What else do you notice? *(The words are not just surface observations; they are deeply personal feelings.)* Do you have any other important reflections? *(The words represent a wide and varied range of responses.)* Which of these feelings are most valid? *(They are all valid. You may want to acknowledge that this is a rhetorical question, but it is important to validate everyone's feelings.)* Where do these feelings come from? *(Personal experiences, stereotypes, etc.)*

4. It's important for teachers and students to acknowledge that these feelings are in the room and that the class need not be afraid of them. Each person should be allowed to enter this conversation wherever they are without being judged or shut down. Everyone needs to feel free to participate without fear of being called racist or given any other label.

5. It is also essential for students to understand that racial epithets and other dehumanizing or violent language are unacceptable and will not be permitted in the classroom. It is the teacher's responsibility to respond immediately to any use of such language with consequences that are appropriate within the context of the school and to make clear to all students that offensive language is unacceptable.

6. Follow this discussion with the short video How to Tell Someone They Sound Racist by New York City hip-hop DJ and blogger Jay Smooth. You can play this video from Jay Smooth's website, illdoctrine.com. Give students an opportunity to discuss their responses, in pairs or as a group. Ask:

- What does Smooth mean by the "what they did" conversation? How is that different from the "what they are" conversation?

- Do you agree with what Smooth suggests when he says that people should focus on "what they did" more than "what they are"? How is the difference important?

- What is the difference between intent and impact? When discussing race and other sensitive issues, is it useful to distinguish between the two?

7. Next, create a classroom contract. Acknowledging that these complicated feelings are in the room and considering what Jay Smooth said, ask students: What do we, as a community of learners, need from each other to have a safe yet courageous conversation about race in this lesson? You can use our Contracting guidelines for creating a classroom contract or another procedure you have used in the past. Make sure that the contract is clear about offensive, dehumanizing, and violent language being unacceptable.

## Addressing Dehumanizing Language

Because Beals is quoting racist protestors, the word "nigger" appears frequently in the text. It is very difficult to use and discuss the term "nigger" in the classroom, but its presence in the memoir makes it necessary to acknowledge it and set guidelines for students about whether or not to pronounce it when reading aloud or quoting from the text. Otherwise, this word's presence might distract students from an open discussion of the events and human behavior. We believe that the best way to prepare to encounter this language is to create a classroom contract outlining guidelines for respectful, reflective classroom discussion.

You may also want to review the following articles to help you determine how to approach the term in your classroom. All of these articles can be found online.

- "Exploring the Controversy: The 'N' Word" from *"Huck Finn" in Context: A Teaching Guide* (PBS)

- "Straight Talk about the N-Word" from *Teaching Tolerance* (Southern Poverty Law Center)

- "In Defense of a Loaded Word" by Ta-Nehisi Coates (*New York Times*)

## Providing Space to Process

We urge teachers to create space for students to have a range of reactions and emotions as they read, and to establish practices in the classroom to reflect on this emotionally powerful material. Below are three strategies that you can use repeatedly during your teaching of the memoir.

1. Exit Cards: Exit cards ask students to briefly respond to a question on a small piece of paper, like an index card, and hand it in before leaving class for the day. These cards offer immediate feedback for teachers about what students are thinking and feeling in response to a lesson or activity. One simple prompt for an exit card is, "What questions, ideas, and feelings did today's class raise for you?"

2. Journals: Journals provide a safe, accessible space for students to share thoughts, feelings, and uncertainties as they work with difficult material. They foster a practice of reflection and document students' evolving thinking. Journal writing can be used as homework to prepare for class discussion; it can also bring valuable moments of silence into the classroom. Any kind of notebook can be used for a journal; what is important is that a student's journal entries are collected together.

There are many different ways to focus students' writing in journals. A few approaches that work include the following:

- **Sentence stems:** "This section of the memoir makes me feel . . . "; "As I read this section of the memoir, I wondered . . . "; "If I could talk with one of the characters in the memoir, I would want to say/I would want to ask . . . "

- **Lifted line responses:** Students select a particular quotation that strikes them and then answer such questions as, "What is interesting to you about this quotation? What does it make you think about? What questions does it raise for you?"

- **Freewriting:** Students use a defined amount of time to write in silence about any aspect of their reading that is on their mind.

3. Color, Symbol, Image: This strategy is adapted from a thinking routine developed by educators at Harvard University's Project Zero. It invites students to reflect on ideas in nonverbal ways and encourages them to think metaphorically. Students first focus on something they've just read and think about the most important theme, idea, or emotion that surfaced for them. Then they reflect on how they can communicate the essence of what they've read using a color, a symbol, and an image.

In this strategy, start by prompting students this way:

Think about the big themes, ideas, or emotions in what you've just read, and select one big idea you'd like to focus on. Then, with that in mind:

- Choose a color that you think best represents that big idea.

- Choose a symbol that you think best represents that idea.

- Choose an image that you think best represents that idea.

Students' responses can be private, or you can apply the Gallery Walk teaching strategy and ask students to reflect on the patterns, similarities, and differences in how they are responding to particular sections of *Warriors Don't Cry*.

# DEFINING SEGREGATION

## Reading Assignment

*Chapters 1–3, pages 1–32 (abridged)*

## Overview

*Warriors Don't Cry* begins with a series of incidents that introduce Melba Pattillo's family—her grandmother India; her mother and father, who divorced when Melba was very young; and her brother Conrad. Many of these incidents detail the injustices and humiliations that Melba and her family experience in Little Rock, Arkansas, in the 1940s and early 1950s. The author recalls in particular the day the Supreme Court rules that separate public schools for Black and white students are illegal. As she walks home from school that day, a white man, angry about the decision, tries to rape her. After much debate, the adults in Melba's family—her parents and grandmother— decide to keep the attack secret. They fear that reporting the matter to the police might result in "something worse" happening.

The author also recounts the day in 1955 when a teacher asks if anyone living in the Central High School district would like to attend the school in the fall of 1957. Melba volunteers without consulting her family. But after reading about attempts to stop integration, she decides that nothing will come of the plan. To her surprise and her family's amazement, Melba is one of the students chosen to integrate Central High School. Although her parents fear the consequences of her participation, they allow Melba to make her own choice.

In preparation for the opening of school, Melba meets with school officials and community leaders like Daisy Bates, the Arkansas president of the NAACP. She also renews her friendship with the eight other African American students who will be attending Central High with her. On Monday, September 2, the day before school is scheduled to begin, Governor Orval E. Faubus suddenly announces that he is sending the Arkansas National Guard to Central High "to maintain order and protect the lives and property" of the citizens of Little Rock. The governor's action delays the arrival of the Black students by one day. That day is spent in court securing an order for integration to proceed as planned. Fearful for the safety of Melba and the other Black students, Daisy Bates asks a few ministers, both Black and white, to accompany the students on their first day of school.

## Pre-Reading Activities

### 1. Introduce the Central Question

Explain that students will be reading about a young African American woman who braved daily harassment when she enrolled at an all-white high school in Little Rock,

Arkansas, in September 1957. The central question will guide students' thinking about what it takes to stand up to racism as they read the memoir.

**Q:** *What can we do, alone and with others, to confront racism? How can we as individuals and as citizens make a positive difference in our school, community, and nation?*

Ask students to read What She Learned and then answer the first two connection questions, either in their journals or in discussion. Students should then articulate their initial thinking about the central question by answering the third connection question in their journals. Remind them that they will return to this question multiple times to add to or revise their thinking as they read the book.

## 2. Define Racism

For at least 400 years, a theory of "race" has been a lens through which many individuals, leaders, and nations have determined who belongs and who does not. The theory is based on the belief that humankind is divided into distinct "races" and that the existence of these races is proven by scientific evidence. Most biologists and geneticists today strongly disagree with this claim. They maintain that there is no genetic or biological basis for categorizing people by race. According to microbiologist Pilar Ossorio:

> Are the people who we call Black more like each other than they are like people who we call white, genetically speaking? The answer is no. There's as much or more diversity and genetic difference within any racial group as there is between people of different racial groups.[1]

Nevertheless, throughout history many societies have not only divided humankind into races but also claimed that some races are permanently and biologically superior to others. This system of beliefs has led to racism. According to scholar George Frederickson, racism has two components: difference and power.

> It originates from a mindset that regards "them" as different from "us" in ways that are permanent and unbridgeable. This sense of difference provides a motive or rationale for using our power advantage to treat the . . . Other in ways that we would regard as cruel or unjust if applied to members of our own group.[2]

Often we can identify racism in specific acts of hate or discrimination carried out by members of a dominant group against those identified as members of particular race. But racism is often less overt. In her book *Why Are All the Black Kids Sitting Together in the Cafeteria?*, Beverly Daniel Tatum does not characterize racism as overt discrimination or individual acts of hate. Rather, she defines it as one's benefiting from a system of privileges based on race that are subtly ingrained in the surrounding culture, making them difficult to detect. It is possible for people of color to be prejudiced on the basis of race, Tatum explains, but the social system is never in their favor. This is racism. She compares racism to smog: "Sometimes it is so thick it is visible, other times it is less apparent, but always, day in and day out, we are breathing it in."[3]

---

1   Pilar Ossorio, *Race: The Power of an Illusion*, Episode 1: "The Difference Between Us" (California Newsreel, 2003), transcript accessed May 2, 2016, http://newsreel.org/transcripts/race1.htm.
2   George M. Fredrickson, *Racism: A Short History* (Princeton, NJ: Princeton University Press, 2002), 9.
3   Beverly Daniel Tatum, *Why Are All the Black Kids Sitting Together in the Cafeteria: And Other Conversations About Race*, rev. ed. (New York: Basic Books, 2003), 6.

Ask students to create a working definition of the word *racism*. A working definition is one that grows and changes as students encounter new information and develop new insights. To help students develop a working definition, ask them to list examples of racism and then determine what the examples have in common. Begin by sharing with students a racist act or circumstance that you have experienced, witnessed, or read about. Explain not only the action or circumstance but also what makes it racist and how you or others responded to it. Did someone take a stand, speak out, or come to the aid of the victim?

Invite students to recall and write in their journals about examples of racism they have witnessed, read about, or experienced. Ask them to tell a partner about the example. Have them describe how they felt about it, the ways they or others responded to it, and what made them believe it was racist. Then have students discuss the following questions with their partners:

- What does each example add to your understanding of the term?

- What do the incidents have in common? To what extent is each unique?

- Do the examples suggest anything about how racism can be overcome?

Students can then craft their working definitions with their partners. Provide some time for each pair to share their definition of racism with the class, and allow students to further refine their definitions as they hear each other's ideas. You might also share the above quotations from Ossorio, Frederickson, and Tatum to help shape students' thinking.

### 3. Provide Context

To provide students with context for *Warriors Don't Cry*, share the video Understanding Jim Crow (see facinghistory.org/warriors-media) and the reading The Road to Little Rock. Use the connection questions following the reading to lead a discussion about the ways that racism can become embedded in society and how it might be confronted.

### 4. Discuss How the Memoir Was Written

As a class, discuss Melba Pattillo Beals's description of how she wrote her memoir over the course of three decades. Ask volunteers to read aloud the reading *Warrior's Don't Cry* Author's Note from the memoir's original edition and then consider the sources of information that Beals used in writing her memoir: the diary she kept as a teenager, newspaper accounts from the period, her own recollections, and those of her mother. Ask students to identify the likely strengths and the possible weaknesses of each source. Use the connection questions that follow the reading to guide the discussion.

## Exploring the Text

Ask students for their questions or comments about what they have read in this section. Then use the following questions as journal or discussion prompts to guide students' exploration of the text.

### Examine the ways segregation defines and confines Melba Pattillo and other African Americans in Little Rock in the 1950s.

1. Melba writes, "Black folks aren't born expecting segregation. . . . Instead the humiliating expectations and traditions of segregation creep over you, slowly stealing a teaspoonful of your self-esteem each day" (page 3, abridged). How does Melba learn those expectations and traditions? What does she know about segregation by the time that she is eight years old? What has she learned by the age of 12?

2. How do the "humiliating expectations and traditions of segregation" shape the attitudes and actions of the adults in Melba's family? How do those expectations and traditions affect the way Melba views these family members' ability to protect her and themselves from mistreatment?

3. In 1954, when Melba is 13, a white man tries to rape her. How do the adults in Melba's family respond to the incident? Why do you think they decide not to call the police? What do they fear? How do these fears affect the way Melba sees herself and others?

4. What does Melba's account suggest about the way racism affects everyone in a society—those who are considered privileged as well as those who are victims of racism? What does it suggest about the way racism threatens democracy?

### Examine Melba's decision to attend Central High.

5. What prompts Melba to raise her hand when a teacher asks who would like to attend Central High? Why do you think she does not tell her family that she has volunteered?

6. How do Melba's parents and grandmother respond to the news that she has been chosen to attend Central High? What do they fear? Why do you think they allow her to attend despite those fears?

7. Superintendent Virgil Blossom and other school officials choose Melba and the other eight African American students to desegregate Central High from dozens of applicants. What do these students have in common? What qualities may have prompted school officials to decide on these particular students?

8. According to the memoir, how do school and community leaders prepare for the desegregation of Central High? Whom do they consult? Whom do they leave out of the process? How important do you think these omissions will be?

9. On September 3, 1957, Governor Orval Faubus told the people of Arkansas, "I must state here in all sincerity, that it is my opinion, yes, even a conviction, that it will not be possible to restore or to maintain order and protect the lives and property of the citizens if forcible integration is carried out tomorrow in the schools of this community" (page 28, abridged). What effect do you think his words will have on Black and white citizens of Little Rock? On people in surrounding communities? What does his statement suggest about the way he defines his role as governor?

**Consider how the author uses stories to introduce readers to members of her family.**

10. How does Melba use anecdotes and other stories to introduce her family to readers?

11. Which members of the family seem the most real to you? Who would you like to know more about?

12. Why do you think that so many of Melba's stories focus on her mother and grandmother?

## Activities for Deeper Understanding

### 1. Use Journals

Encourage students to keep a journal as they read *Warriors Don't Cry*. Unlike a finished work, a journal documents the process of thinking. In addition to using their journals to capture their reflections as they read, suggest that students respond to the following journal prompts:

- Write your responses to the story so far. You might also list questions and comments that come to mind as you read the book.

- Create a timeline to show what has happened in the story. Pay particular attention to the events that take place at the beginning of the 1957–1958 school year. Add to the timeline as you continue reading.

- List the ways that the author and her family confront or respond to racism in Little Rock. Which strategies are most effective? Least effective?

- As Melba prepares for her first day at Central High, what does she seem to be most excited about? What does she fear? What do you think her first day will be like?

### 2. Metaphors and Merry-Go-Rounds

Remind students that a *metaphor* is a figure of speech that compares two seemingly unlike things without the use of such comparative words as *like* or *as*. When Melba writes, "For me, Cincinnati was the promised land," she is using a metaphor. To what is she comparing Cincinnati? How are the two places alike in her view?

Distribute copies of the poem Merry-Go-Round. Tell students that this poem by Langston Hughes uses a carousel as a metaphor. Ask a volunteer to read the poem aloud. Then have students work with a partner to decide what is being compared to the merry-go-round. Students might also consider how the incident described in the poem is like Melba's encounter with the operator of a carousel (page 4, abridged). What do the two encounters add to our understanding of a segregated society? To our understanding of racism?

# Extension Activities

### 1. Rosa Parks and the Montgomery Bus Boycott

Explain the importance of another watershed moment in civil rights history. Distribute copies of the reading Rosa Parks and the Montgomery Boycott and use the connection questions either as journal prompts or for classroom discussion.

### 2. Growing Up in the South

You may wish to encourage students to read and report on an autobiography of an African American who grew up in the 1940s and 1950s. Possibilities include Julius Lester, Marian Wright Edelman, Gloria Wade, Maya Angelou, and Malcolm X. Discuss how the experiences of the chosen individual are similar to those described in *Warriors Don't Cry*. What differences are most striking?

# What She Learned

On page 222 of the abridged edition of *Warriors Don't Cry*, Melba Pattillo Beals reflects on what she learned from the choices she made during the 1957–1958 school year as one of the first nine African American students at Central High School:

> I look back on my Little Rock experience as ultimately a positive force that shaped the course of my life. As Grandma India promised, it taught me to have courage and patience.
>
> My Central High School experience also taught me that we are not separate. The effort to separate ourselves whether by race, creed, color, religion, or status is as costly to the separator as to those who would be separated. . . .
>
> The task that remains is to cope with our interdependence—to see ourselves reflected in every other human being and to respect and honor our differences.

## Connection Questions

1. What did Melba learn from her experience during her year at Central High?

2. How does Melba think we can best respond to the differences between us?

3. Throughout your reading of *Warriors Don't Cry*, you will return to the central question below and record how your thinking about it has changed:

   **Q:** *What can we do, alone and with others, to confront racism? How can we as individuals and as citizens make a positive difference in our school, community, and nation?*

Based on her reflection above, how might Melba answer this question? Write down your own first thoughts in response to this question.

# The Road to Little Rock

Melba Pattillo was born at a time in history when, in the words of historian Lerone Bennett, Jr., "America was two nations—one white, one black, separate and unequal." He likens the segregation that marked that era to "a wall, a system, a way of separating people from people." That wall did not go up in a single day. It was built—"brick by brick, bill by bill, fear by fear." In the 1940s and early 1950s, when Melba Pattillo was growing up in Arkansas, that wall seemed almost impenetrable. Yet during those years, a few Americans, both Black and white, were chipping away at segregation—little by little, step by step. A major victory came on Monday, May 17, 1954.

On that day, Chief Justice Earl Warren delivered the United States Supreme Court's unanimous decision in a case known as *Brown v. Board of Education of Topeka.* The ruling overturned nearly 60 years of forced segregation in many of the nation's schools. The justices argued that separating some children from others solely on account of their race "generates a feeling of inferiority as to their status in the community that may affect their hearts and minds in a way unlikely ever to be undone." They declared that "in the field of public education the doctrine of 'separate but equal' has no place. Separate educational facilities are inherently unequal. . . . Therefore, we hold that the plaintiffs and others similarly situated . . . are . . . deprived of the equal protection of the laws guaranteed by the Fourteenth Amendment."

The Fourteenth Amendment was passed in 1866 and ratified in 1868, three years after the Thirteenth Amendment abolished slavery. The Fourteenth Amendment was added to the Constitution to protect the rights of formerly enslaved African Americans. For the first time in American history, they were regarded as citizens of the United States equal to any other citizen. The amendment defines a US citizen as a person "born or naturalized in the United States, and subject to the jurisdiction thereof." It declares that no state may pass laws that "abridge the privileges or immunities of citizens of the United States," deprive "any person of life, liberty or property, without due process of law," or deny "to any person within its jurisdiction the equal protection of the laws."

## The Growth of Segregation

Despite the Fourteenth Amendment, the rights of African Americans in the late 1800s were constantly under attack almost everywhere in the nation, but most particularly in the South. For example, in 1883 the Supreme Court ruled that the Civil Rights Act of 1875, which outlawed discrimination, was unconstitutional because it violated the right of businesses, institutions, and civic organizations to choose their customers, employees, and/or members. The justices claimed that the Fourteenth Amendment applied only to state governments.

A few years later, an African American named Homer Plessy challenged segregation on streetcars in his home state of Louisiana. He claimed that it violated his rights as a citizen of the United States. In 1896, in the case of *Plessy v. Ferguson,* the United States Supreme Court ruled against Plessy. Eight of the nine justices maintained that separate facilities for Blacks do not violate the rights of Black Americans as long as their facilities are equal to those provided for whites. Only one justice disagreed. In his dissent, John Marshall Harlan, a former slaveholder from Kentucky, wrote, "In respect of civil rights, all citizens are equal before the law. The humblest is the peer of the most powerful. The law regards man as man, and takes no account of his surroundings or of his color when his civil rights as guaranteed by the supreme law of the land are involved." Nearly 60 years would pass before the Supreme Court heeded Harlan's words.

The decision in *Plessy v. Ferguson* permitted the growth of a system of state and local laws known as "Jim Crow" laws. They established racial barriers in almost every aspect of life. In many places, Black and white Americans could not publicly eat, travel, or sit side by side. Churches, schools, movie theaters, and even cemeteries were segregated.

## Challenging Segregation

Over the years, Americans formed a number of organizations to oppose segregation. Among them was the National Association for the Advancement of Colored People (the NAACP). Its founders included both Black and white Americans. In 1935, the group set into motion a plan to systematically challenge Jim Crow in court by inviting Professor Charles Houston of Howard University Law School to become its chief counsel. Soon after, Thurgood Marshall, a former student, joined him. The two lawyers, along with other civil rights attorneys, initially focused their efforts on segregation in higher education, because they knew that few states could afford "separate but equal" legal, medical, and other professional training for their Black and white students.

Slowly, the NAACP's legal team made progress. In 1949, the Supreme Court ruled that a Texas law school set up only for African American students did not meet the standard of equality because of "those qualities which are incapable of objective measurement but which make for the greatness in a law school" (*Sweatt v. Painter*). In a 1950 decision (*McLaurin v. Oklahoma*), the justices concluded that an African American student at the University of Oklahoma was not receiving an education equal to that of white students as long as he was segregated in the classroom, cafeteria, and library. The court ruled that "such restrictions impair and inhibit his ability to study, engage in discussions and exchange views with other students, and in general, to learn his profession."

Little by little, ruling by ruling, the wall that separated Americans was coming down. After chipping away at segregation in higher education, NAACP lawyers turned their attention to segregation in the nation's public schools. This time they supported cases filed in four states and the District of Columbia. Each challenged the constitutionality of separating children by race. In late 1952, the justices decided that the cases were so similar that they should be heard together. So they combined them into a single case, which came to be known as *Brown v. Board of Education of Topeka, et al.* The Supreme Court's decision came in May 1954. The following September, the first African American students enrolled in formerly all-white schools in Washington, DC, and 150 school districts in eight states, including Arkansas. At the same time, a number of people in the South organized groups opposing integration.

When the Supreme Court issued its decision in the *Brown* case, the justices did not provide guidelines for ending segregation in the nation's public schools. They waited until May 31, 1955, to rule that the federal courts were to decide whether a school district was acting in "good faith" by desegregating its schools "with all deliberate speed." Among the few Southern governors to applaud the decision was Orval Faubus of Arkansas.

Some school boards in Arkansas issued plans for desegregation even before the Supreme Court issued its second decision. Others, like the Little Rock School Board, drew up a plan in response to the ruling. As required by the Supreme Court, a federal district court reviewed the Little Rock plan and approved it as a "good faith" effort. Between 1955 and 1957, the year it was to go into effect, Virgil Blossom, the superintendent of schools, presented the plan to dozens of civic groups, PTAs, and other organizations in the white community. Voters had a say in the plan, as well. In the spring of 1957, it was an issue in the election of the Little Rock School Board. For the most part, the winners in that election supported the plan. Despite the protests of a few noisy segregationists, many people in Little Rock and elsewhere were confident that the plan would be implemented peacefully with little or no conflict.

## Connection Questions

1. How was racism embedded into everyday life in the United States in the 1940s and 1950s?

2. What is the doctrine of "separate but equal"? What was the Supreme Court's ruling on that doctrine in 1896? How did the court's ruling change in 1954? What reasoning did Justice Warren offer for the 1954 decision?

3. What strategy did the NAACP lawyers use to chip away at segregation before the *Brown v. Board of Education* ruling? What was the impact of the *Brown* decision?

4. What does the history summarized in this reading suggest about how individuals and groups can make positive change in society?

# *Warriors Don't Cry* Author's Note

When *Warriors Don't Cry* was first published in 1994, it was accompanied by the following author's note:

> Although this happened over thirty-five years ago, I remember being inside Central High School as though it were yesterday. Memories leap out in a heartbeat, summoned by the sound of a helicopter, the wrath in a shouting voice, or the expression on a scowling face.
>
> From the beginning I kept a diary, and my mother, Dr. Lois Pattillo, a high school English teacher, kept copious notes and clipped a sea of newspaper articles. I began the first draft of this book when I was eighteen, but in the ensuing years, I could not face the ghosts its pages called up. During the intervals of renewed strength and commitment, I would find myself compelled to return to the manuscript, only to have the pain of reliving my past undo my good intentions. Now enough time has elapsed to allow healing to take place, enabling me to tell my story without bitterness.
>
> In some instances I have changed people's names to protect their identities. But all the incidents recounted here are based on the diary I kept, on news clippings, and on the recollections of my family and myself. While some of the conversations have been re-created, the story is accurate and conveys my truth of what it was like to live in the midst of a civil rights firestorm.[1]

## Connection Questions

1. What did Melba learn from her experience during her year at Central High?

2. How does Melba think we can best respond to the differences between us?

---

1  Melba Pattillo Beals, *Warriors Don't Cry: A Searing Memoir of the Battle to Integrate Little Rock's Central High* (New York: Washington Square Press, 1994), xx.

# Merry-Go-Round

Langston Hughes was one of the nation's best-known African American writers in the first half of the twentieth century. He wrote this poem, called "Merry-Go-Round," in the 1950s.

*Colored child at carnival:*

Where is the Jim Crow section
On this merry-go-round,
Mister, cause I want to ride?
Down South where I come from
White and colored
Can't sit side by side.
Down South on the train
There's a Jim Crow car.
On the bus we're put in the back—
But there ain't no back
To a merry-go-round!
Where's the horse
For a kid that's black?[1]

## Connection Questions

1. How do you think the carousel operator will answer the child's question?

2. What problems does the poem suggest that merry-go-rounds or carousels present in a segregated society?

1  Langston Hughes, "Merry-Go-Round," in *Don't You Turn Back: Poems by Langston Hughes*, ed. Lee Bennett Hopkins (New York: Alfred A. Knopf, 1969).

# Rosa Parks and the Montgomery Boycott

At a time when Melba Pattillo believed that it would take a miracle to end segregation in Little Rock, such a miracle was taking place in Montgomery, Alabama. On Thursday, December 1, 1955, Rosa Parks, a 42-year-old African American woman, boarded a city bus at the end of a hard day's work. As the seats in the white section filled up, the driver ordered Blacks near the front of the bus to move farther back. Only Parks refused. The driver responded by calling the police, who immediately placed her under arrest.

Rosa Parks was not acting on a whim. As a member of the National Association for the Advancement of Colored People (the NAACP), she and others were actively seeking opportunities to challenge segregation. When news of Parks's arrest spread through the Black community, a number of individuals and groups quickly took action. The first to do so was the Women's Political Council, a Black professional organization. Members organized a boycott of the city buses to show support for Parks and opposition to segregation. The women worked through the night, making 35,000 copies of a leaflet that urged Blacks to stay off the buses. That same day, a group of Black ministers and other leaders met to consider their response to Parks's arrest. They decided to support the women's boycott.

On Monday, December 5, over 90% of the African Americans in Montgomery who regularly rode the buses walked, joined carpools, or drove horse-drawn wagons to get to work. That evening, a young Baptist minister named Martin Luther King Jr. reminded a crowd of over 5,000 Blacks that "first and foremost we are American citizens." He told them, "The only weapon we have . . . is the weapon of protest," and "the great glory of American democracy is the right to protest for right."[1] That right to nonviolent protest is protected by the First Amendment to the Constitution.

For 383 days, African Americans in Montgomery refused to take the bus. They ignored harassment, threats, and intimidation. They also supported a lawsuit charging that Rosa Parks should not have been arrested because segregated public buses are unconstitutional.

The boycott finally ended on December 20, 1956, when city officials received a direct order from the United States Supreme Court that called for an end to segregation on public transportation in the city. The next morning, Martin Luther King and Rosa Parks were among the first African Americans to board Montgomery's newly integrated buses. Against all odds, African Americans in Montgomery had challenged the system and won.

---

1    Martin Luther King Jr., "Address to the first Montgomery Improvement Association (MIA) Mass Meeting, December 5, 1955," *King Encyclopedia* website (Stanford University King Institute), http://kingencyclopedia.stanford.edu/encyclopedia/documentsentry/the_addres_to_the_first_montgomery_improvement_association_mia_mass_meeting.1.html.

## Connection Questions

1. What does the boycott suggest about the power of ordinary people to make a difference? What impact and effects can a boycott have?

2. A boycott is one example of a nonviolent protest. Name other examples of nonviolent protest. How important are these forms of protest in a democracy?

3. Why do you think Melba experienced a "surge of pride when I thought about how my people had banded together to force a change"?

4. In what ways is this incident related to the experiences and events in Little Rock, Arkansas?

# BECOMING A "WARRIOR"

## Reading Assignment

*Chapters 4–8, pages 33–68 (abridged)*

## Overview

On Wednesday, September 4, Melba and the other eight African American students are scheduled to walk to school with several ministers. As Melba and her mother head for the place where the group is to meet, they spot one of Melba's friends, Elizabeth Eckford, standing alone with a line of soldiers in front of her and an angry mob at her back. Unable to get past the soldiers, Elizabeth retreats to a bus stop even as the crowd continues to heckle and taunt her. When a few men in the crowd threaten Melba and her mother, the two quickly flee the area.

Melba's shaken mother tells Melba to keep their experience a secret. She also urges her daughter to return to her segregated school, but Melba's grandmother counsels persistence. As Melba is grappling with her own fears and disappointment, her grandmother tells her, "You're a warrior on the battlefield for your Lord. God's warriors don't cry, 'cause they trust that he's always by their side." Melba decides to remain at Central High, but it will be 17 days before she is able to do so.

For over two weeks, city and state leaders argue over whether integration ought to proceed as planned. Although Melba feels lonely and uncertain, she finds comfort in the support of her church and the many volunteers who keep her and the others from falling behind in their studies. Finally, on Friday, September 20, a federal judge orders the governor to stop interfering with integration. Faubus responds by removing the National Guard. The following Monday, Melba and the other eight students are to return to school.

## Exploring the Text

Ask students for their questions or comments about what they have read in this section. Then use the following questions as journal or discussion prompts to guide students' exploration of the text.

### Discuss how secrets affect Melba's view of herself and her family.

1. Why does Melba's mother insist that she and Melba keep their encounter with the mob outside Central High School a secret, even if it means telling a "white lie"? What is a "white lie"? How is it different from other lies?

2. How does keeping the secret affect Melba in the weeks that follow?

3. What other secrets has Melba kept over the years? How do those secrets shape the way she sees herself and her family?

### Consider what it means to be a "warrior on the battlefield for your Lord."

4. Melba's grandmother likens Melba to a "warrior on the battlefield for your Lord." What is a *warrior*? How is a "warrior for one's Lord" different from other warriors?

5. In what sense are Melba and the other eight students "warriors"? What qualities do warriors have? Which of those qualities do you think they will need to make it through the school year?

6. Do you agree with the advice Melba's grandmother gives her? When is crying a sign of weakness? A sign of strength? Who decides? Is it different for men? For women? For children?

### Describe how the crisis at Central High School affects people in Little Rock and other places.

7. How does Melba characterize the way that individuals and groups in Little Rock, both Black and white, respond to the crisis?

8. What role does the media seem to play in the crisis? How important is that role?

9. On page 52 of the abridged edition, Melba describes an ad created by a white man from a small town in Arkansas. What is the message of his ad? At whom is it directed? How do you explain Melba's response to it? How do you think others in the community may have responded?

### Explore the way that Melba uses comparison and contrasts to show the effects of segregation.

10. What qualities does Melba attribute to Thurgood Marshall? Which of these qualities does she most admire?

11. To which adults does she compare Marshall? What does that comparison suggest about the way she views those adults?

12. What does her comparison suggest about the effects of segregation?

## Connecting to the Central Question

After exploring the text and reviewing the events that take place in this section of the book, provide students with an opportunity to revisit their initial thinking about this guide's central question:

**Q:** *What can we do, alone and with others, to confront racism? How can we as individuals and as citizens make a positive difference in our school, community, and nation?*

Give students a few minutes to write down their thoughts in response to this question in light of what they have learned about Melba's experiences while trying to enter Central High School in September 1957. In what ways has the author and her family confronted racism in this section of the book? Which strategies are most effective? Least effective?

# Activities for Deeper Understanding

## 1. Explore Multiple Perspectives

By exploring multiple perspectives on an incident, students develop a more nuanced understanding of that event. Start by asking a volunteer to read aloud Melba's account of Elizabeth Eckford's ordeal on September 4, 1957 (abridged, pages 36–37). Then have students explore additional descriptions of these events (perhaps using the Jigsaw teaching strategy).

- Review Elizabeth's memories of that day, either by distributing the reading In Elizabeth Eckford's Words or by playing the audio version (see facinghistory.org /warriors-media) of her recollections.

- Read the recollections of other witnesses featured in the reading Crisis in Little Rock.

- If you have access to the series *Eyes on the Prize: America's Civil Rights Years*, you can also show the first 30 minutes of Episode 2: "Fighting Back (1957–62)." It uses interviews and television footage to tell Elizabeth's story.

After reviewing the different accounts, discuss the similarities and differences between them and the one in *Warriors Don't Cry*. How do students account for differences? What questions would they have asked if they had been reporters at the school that day?

## 2. Rewrite a Wrong

In 1987, Elizabeth Eckford said of her ordeal, "I remember this tremendous feeling of being alone and I didn't know how I was going to get out of there. I didn't know whether I would be injured. There was this deafening roar. I could hear individual voices, but I was not conscious of numbers, I was conscious of being alone."

Ask students to revisit the descriptions of the incident from the last activity (including taking a second look at the television footage of Elizabeth Eckford included in *Eyes on the Prize: America's Civil Rights Years*, Episode 2: "Fighting Back (1957–62)" if you have access to it). Also refer students to the famous photograph of Elizabeth Eckford and Hazel Bryan and apply the Analyzing Images teaching strategy. How did the crowd physically and emotionally isolate Eckford? What part did the soldiers play in her isolation?

Then have students write a paragraph describing what might have happened if various individuals or groups had come to Elizabeth's aid. For example, what if the principal or a group of teachers had opened the doors of the school and escorted Elizabeth into the building? Elizabeth lived in an integrated neighborhood near Central High School. She knew a number of white students. What if a few of those students had joined her as she sat on the bench? What if the mayor of Little Rock or the superintendent of schools had accompanied her to school that day? In what ways could it have altered the outcome of that day? How do you think Elizabeth would have felt?

### 3. Journal Prompts

In addition to responding to the reading selection and continuing to add to their time-lines, suggest that students respond to one or more of the following writing prompts:

- Melba reflects on the meaning of the word *freedom*. How are her experiences at Central High altering or deepening her understanding of the term? What does the word *freedom* mean to you? What experiences have shaped your understanding of it?

- What changes do you detect in Melba in this part of the story? To what extent is she finding her voice?

- Write an account of the events that take place at Central High on the morning of September 4, 1957, from the viewpoint of someone who is watching those events on TV.

- What do you think Melba's first day of classes at Central High will be like? Record your predictions and then check them as you read the next section of the book.

## Extension Activity

### Where Were the Adults?

Encourage interested students to follow the events in Little Rock through the eyes of an adult who was there at the time. Daisy Bates, the president of the Arkansas NAACP; Elizabeth Huckaby, a vice principal at Central High; Harry Ashmore, the editor of the *Arkansas Gazette*; and Virgil Blossom, the superintendent of the Little Rock Public Schools, have all written books about that year:

- *The Long Shadow of Little Rock* by Daisy Bates

- *Crisis at Central High, Little Rock, 1957–58* by Elizabeth Huckaby

- *Civil Rights and Wrongs* by Harry S. Ashmore

- *It Has Happened Here* by Virgil T. Blossom

Hold a panel discussion to compare and contrast their perspectives with Melba Pattillo Beals's.

# In Elizabeth Eckford's Words

I am Elizabeth Eckford. I am part of the group that became known as the Little Rock Nine. Prior to the [de]segregation of Central, there had been one high school for whites, Central High School; one high school for blacks, Dunbar. I expected that there may be something more available to me at Central that was not available at Dunbar; that there might be more courses I could pursue; that there were more options available. I was not prepared for what actually happened.

I was more concerned about what I would wear, whether we could finish my dress in time . . . was that okay, would it look good. The night before, when the governor went on television and announced that he had called out the Arkansas National Guard, I thought that he had done this to ensure the protection of all the students. We did not have a telephone, so inadvertently we were not contacted to let us know that Daisy Bates of NAACP had arranged for some ministers to accompany the students in a group. And so it was that I arrived alone.

On the morning of September 4th, my mother was doing what she usually did. My mother was making sure everybody's hair looked right and everybody had their lunch money and their notebooks and things. But she did finally get quiet and we had family prayer. I remember my father walking back and forth. My father worked at night and normally he would have been asleep at that time, but he was awake and he was walking back and forth chomping on a cigar that wasn't lit.

I expected that I would go to school as before on a city bus. So, I walked a few blocks to the bus stop, got on the bus, and rode to within two blocks of the school. I got off the bus and I noticed along the street that there were many more cars than usual. And I remember hearing the murmur of a crowd. But when I got to the corner where the school was, I was reassured seeing these soldiers circling the school grounds. And I saw students going to school. I saw the guards break ranks as students approached the sidewalks so that they could pass through to get to school. And I approached the guard at the corner as I had seen some other students do and they closed ranks. So I thought, "Maybe I am not supposed to enter at this point." So I walked further down the line of guards to where there was another sidewalk and I attempted to pass through there. But when I stepped up, they crossed rifles. And again I said to myself, "So maybe I'm supposed to go down to where the main entrance is." So I walked toward the center of the street and when I got to about the middle and I approached the guard, he directed me across the street *into the crowd*. It was only then that I realized that they were barring me, that I wouldn't go to school.

As I stepped out into the street, the people who had been across the street started surging forward behind me. So I headed in the opposite direction to where there was another bus stop. Safety to me meant getting to that bus stop. It seemed like I sat there for a long time before the bus came. In the meantime, people were screaming behind me. What I would have described as a crowd before, to my ears sounded like a mob.[1]

---

1   From an interview with Facing History and Ourselves, 1997.

# Crisis in Little Rock

As fall neared, resistance to integration became more vocal in Little Rock and elsewhere. A number of African American students responded by withdrawing their applications. By the time school opened, only nine were prepared to attend Central High School—Minnijean Brown, Elizabeth Eckford, Ernest Green, Thelma Mothershed, Melba Pattillo, Gloria Ray, Terrence Roberts, Jefferson Thomas, and Carlotta Walls. Despite the talk on TV, over the radio, and in the newspapers, they did not believe that integration would lead to violence in Little Rock.

Ernest Green recalls:

> There hadn't been any trouble expected, given the fact that there had been other schools in Arkansas that had been integrated—Fort Smith, Arkansas, and some others. The buses in Little Rock had been desegregated without any problem. The library was integrated, the medical school, and the law school at the University had admitted some blacks. So there was an expectation that there would be minimal problems, but nothing major that would put Little Rock on the map. The first inclination that I had of it was the night before we were to go to school, the Labor Day Monday night. [Governor] Orval Faubus came on TV and indicated that he was calling out the [Arkansas] National Guard to prevent our entrance into Central because of what he thought were threats to our lives. He was doing it for our own "protection." Even at that time that was his line. He said that the troops would be out in front of the school and they would bar our entrance to Central—for our protection as well as for the protection and tranquility of the city.[1]

Tuesday morning, school officials asked the "Little Rock Nine" to stay home while they sought guidance from District Judge Ronald N. Davies. He ordered integration to proceed as planned. The nine Black students were told to report to Central High the next morning. Fearful for the students' safety, Daisy Bates, the president of the Arkansas NAACP, suggested that they come to school as a group. She asked white and Black religious leaders to accompany them.

Fifteen-year-old Elizabeth Eckford knew nothing of the plan. In her haste, Daisy Bates forgot to get word to her. So, early Wednesday morning, Eckford set off for school alone.

When she reached Central High, she found herself surrounded by an angry crowd. As they screamed and threatened, she tried to enter the building, only to be turned away by soldiers armed with bayonets. Unsure what to do and terrified by the mob, Eckford quickly headed for a bus stop even as the crowd continued to spit and scream, taunt and jeer. She later said of her ordeal, "I remember this tremendous feeling of being alone, and I didn't know how I was going to get out of there. I didn't know whether I would be injured. There was this deafening roar. I could hear individual voices, but I was not conscious of numbers. I was conscious of being alone."

A few minutes later, as a second Black student, Terrence Roberts, approached the school, the soldiers formed a human fence to keep him out. Although the crowd taunted Roberts, it was Eckford who bore the brunt of their anger. As she sat on a

---

1  Ernest Green, *Voices of Freedom: An Oral History of the Civil Rights Movement from the 1950s through the 1980s*, ed. Henry Hampton and Steve Fayer (New York: Bantam Books, 1990), 39.

bench with tears streaming down her face, Benjamin Fine of the *New York Times* tried to comfort her. Then a white woman, Grace Lorch, suddenly confronted the mob. Fine reported:

> "She's scared," Mrs. Lorch said. "She's just a little girl." She appealed to the men and women around her.
>
> "Why don't you calm down?" she asked. "I'm not here to fight with you. Six months from now you'll be ashamed at what you're doing."
>
> "Go home, you're just one of them," Mrs. Lorch was told.
>
> She escorted the Negro student to the other side of the street, but the crowd followed.
>
> "Won't somebody please call a taxi?" she pleaded. She was met with hoot calls and jeers.
>
> Finally, after being jostled by the crowd, she worked her way to the street corner, and the two boarded a bus.
>
> Seven other Negro students tried to get into the school. They came together, accompanied by four white ministers. Dunbar Ogden, president of the Greater Little Rock Ministerial Association, acted as spokesman for the group.
>
> "Sorry, we cannot admit Negro students," the officers of the militia told them.
>
> The crowd began to disperse slowly. Many of the students who had waited outside the school building to see whether the Negroes would enter started to go into school. They had said that if the Negroes went in, they would go out.[2]

2   Benjamin Fine, "Arkansas Troops Bar Negro Pupils; Governor Defiant," *New York Times*, September 5, 1957.

## Elizabeth Eckford and Hazel Bryan

**Photographer Will Counts captures 15-year-old Hazel Bryan's reaction to Elizabeth Eckford's presence at Central High in Little Rock, September 4, 1957.**

# INSIDE CENTRAL HIGH

**Reading Assignment**

*Chapters 7–8, pages 69–106 (abridged)*

## Overview

On Monday morning, September 23, Melba and the other eight African American students enter Central High School for the first time. They are hurried in through a side entrance to avoid the mob that has gathered in front of the school. Once inside the building, the nine are sent their separate ways. Melba is harassed in some of her classes and supported in others. Her school day ends abruptly when the police can no longer control the mob outside the school. To protect the nine, Assistant Police Chief Gene Smith leads them through the basement of the school to two waiting cars. Only after she arrives safely at home does Melba learn from news broadcasts that the mob went on a rampage just after she and the others left the building, attacking reporters and breaking windows.

Outraged by the violence, President Dwight D. Eisenhower sends federal troops to Arkansas to protect the nine students. On Wednesday, September 25, soldiers from the 101st Airborne Division escort Melba and the others to school. A soldier is assigned to guard each student during the school day. Danny, Melba's bodyguard, is a reassuring presence as she makes her way to and from classes. But he cannot prevent the harassment she experiences during classes, in study hall, or inside the girls' washroom.

## Exploring the Text

Ask students for their questions or comments about what they have read in this section. Then use the following questions as journal or discussion prompts to guide students' exploration of the text.

### Explore the role of leaders in a crisis.

1. How do the adults at Central High—the principal, vice principal, teachers—respond to the arrival of the African American students? What effect do their responses have on Melba and the other African American students? What effect do you think they have on white students at Central High?

2. At the end of her first day at Central High, Melba decides to include two white men in her prayers. Who are the two men? What distinguishes them from the other white men and women Melba encounters that day?

3. What are the qualities of a good leader? Which of those qualities are particularly valuable during times of crisis and change? Who do you think displays those qualities during the crisis at Central High?

4. It has been said that some leaders make history, others are made by history, and still others are run over by history. Into which category would you place President Eisenhower? Governor Faubus? What qualities does each show in the crisis?

### Explore the various ways individuals respond to change.

5. Describe the range of responses to integration among the white students at Central High.

6. What part do you think peer pressure plays in determining how the white students respond to the African American students?

7. Describe the range of responses among the adults at Central High. What factors may be prompting their responses? For example, what part may prejudice play? What about fears of the mob outside the school? Peer pressure?

### Consider how Melba begins to change.

8. What do Melba's remarks about feeling both proud and sad while being escorted into the school by federal troops (abridged page 95) indicate about her sense of herself as an individual and as a citizen?

9. How do Melba's dealings with the press help her find her voice? What other experiences contribute to a feeling that she can make a difference or that her opinion matters? What experiences undermine that feeling?

## Connecting to the Central Question

After exploring the text and reviewing the events that take place in this section of the book, provide students with an opportunity to revisit their thinking about this guide's central question:

*Q: What can we do, alone and with others, to confront racism? How can we as individuals and as citizens make a positive difference in our school, community, and nation?*

Give students a few minutes to write down their thoughts in response to this question in light of what they have learned about Melba's first days at Central High School in September 1957. In what ways do individuals in this section of the book confront racism? Who responds to the integration of Central High in hateful and threatening ways? Who looks the other way? What factors seem to motivate the variety of choices individuals are making?

## Activities for Deeper Understanding

### 1. The Power of Bystanders

Only a handful of students harassed the African American students. A famous photograph of Elizabeth Eckford shows one of those students. Refer students to this photograph of Elizabeth Eckford and Hazel Bryan on page 28 in Section 2. Photographer Will Counts captured 15-year-old Hazel Bryan with her mouth open and her face distorted with hate. Elizabeth Huckaby, the vice principal at Central High, was haunted by the photo. She later wrote:

> No one seemed to be able to identify the girl—and small wonder. We were not used to seeing our students look like that. But by noon on Friday, I discovered she was someone I knew, and I sent for her in the afternoon. When she readily admitted she was the screaming girl, I told her how distressed I was to hear it since hatred destroys the people who hate. She shrugged. Well, that was the way she felt, she said. Undeterred by her shrug, I said that I hoped I'd never see her pretty face so distorted again, that I never would have recognized that ugly face in the picture as hers. Wasted breath.[1]

Five years later, in 1962, Bryan apologized to Eckford. Bryan later told an interviewer:

> I don't know what triggered it, but one day I just started squalling about how she must have felt. I felt so bad that I had done this that I called her . . . and apologized to her. I told her I was sorry that I had done that, that I was not thinking for myself. . . . I think both of us were crying.[2]

The vast majority of students did not harass Eckford or the other African American students. They were bystanders.

Ask students to read A Bystander at Central High and answer the questions that follow the short reading in their journals. Then discuss as a class. Many sociologists believe that bystanders can influence an event through the attention they pay to that event.

- What messages were students like Marcia Webb sending through their silence? To what extent were they cooperating in the violence?

- Have students compare Webb's response with that of Robin Woods. What similarities do they notice? What differences seem most striking?

## 2. Journal Prompts

In addition to continuing to record their responses to the reading (and adding to their timelines), suggest that students respond to one or more of the following writing prompts:

- Write a summary of Melba's first days at Central High. What has she gained? What has she lost?

- Suppose someone like Robin Woods had been in one of Melba's classes. What difference might it have made to Melba? To the white students?

- How do you think you would feel if soldiers or police officers had to guard you on your way to school or protect you while you were in school?

---

1  Elizabeth Huckaby, *Crisis at Central High, Little Rock, 1957–58* (Baton Rouge: Louisiana State University Press, 1980), 24.
2  Sara Alderman Murphy, *Breaking the Silence: Little Rock's Women's Emergency Committee to Open Our Schools, 1958–1963* (Fayetteville: University of Arkansas Press, 1997), 58.

# Extension Activity

## The President vs. the Governor

Have students contrast the thoughts and actions of President Eisenhower and those of Governor Faubus, which they discussed in the last section. Distribute the reading The President vs. the Governor and use the connection questions for classroom discussion.

# A Bystander at Central High

Marcia Webb was a student at Central High in 1957. As an adult, she reflected on what it meant to be a bystander at that time:

> The things that I thought about when I was in high school were . . . the things that most kids did in the 50s . . . the football team . . . dances. . . . I think it was a white person's world—probably a white man's world. Most of the blacks you had any contact with in 1957 were your household workers, sanitation department helpers, and that would be the only contact you would have. But I remember the picture in the newspaper of Elizabeth Eckford with the jeering white faces behind her. And at that moment I thought, Marcie, you were there and you never once thought about what was going on with Elizabeth Eckford. You were glad there weren't any violent demonstrations, you were glad no one was hurt physically. But then I realized what hurt can come from words, from silence even, from just being ignored. And when I think about it now I think about it with regret. I'm sorry to say now looking back that what was happening didn't have more significance and I didn't take more of an active role. But I was interested in the things that most kids are.[1]

## Connection Questions

1. There is an old saying that "sticks and stones can break my bones but names can never hurt me." Is it true? What is the hurt that comes from words? From silence? From "just being ignored"?

2. How might the situation at Central High School have been different if Webb and other white students had regarded Eckford as a "kid" much like themselves?

3. Like Marcia Webb, Robin Woods was also a student at Central High. She made a very different choice. Terrence Roberts, one of the Little Rock Nine, was in her algebra class. Realizing he didn't yet have a math book, she made "a gut-level decision" and pulled her desk over to his so they could share her book. There was "a gasp of disbelief" in the classroom. For the rest of the year, segregationists harassed Woods and her family. How might the situation at Central High have been different if more students had acted the way Woods did?

1  Joan I. Duffy, "A Reunion with History: Central High Will Observe 1957's Rite of Passage," *Memphis Commercial Appeal*, September 21, 1997.

# The President vs. the Governor

Dwight Eisenhower was born in 1890. He grew up in a segregated society and served for over 30 years in a segregated army. Not long after the *Brown* decision, he told reporters, "You can't change people's hearts merely by laws." He also informed them that he could not imagine a situation in which he would use federal troops to enforce integration. His words delighted segregationists.

Yet after watching the rioting in Little Rock on TV on September 23, Eisenhower ordered federal troops to the city to enforce the law. He told the American people, "Our personal opinions about the [*Brown*] decision have no bearing on the matter of enforcement. . . . Mob rule cannot be allowed to override the decisions of our courts."[1]

On October 5, 1957, the editors of the *Amsterdam News*, an African American newspaper in New York, said of Eisenhower's decision:

> It is not too difficult for a man to stand up and fight for a cause which he himself believes to be right. But it is quite another thing for a man to stand up and fight for a cause with which he himself does not agree but which he feels it is his duty to uphold.
>
> President Eisenhower is a battle-scarred veteran of many a campaign who has been hailed from one end of the world to the other. But we submit that his victory over himself at Little Rock was indeed his finest hour.[2]

## Connection Questions

1. How did the president define his responsibilities?

2. What prompted his decision to send in the troops?

3. Why did the editors of the *Amsterdam News* regard Eisenhower's decision as "his finest hour"? What are they suggesting about the role of a leader? What do you think is the role of a leader in a democracy? What is the role of a citizen?

1  Dwight D. Eisenhower, "Televised Address to the Nation on the Situation in Little Rock" (speech, September 24, 1957), Dwight D. Eisenhower Memorial website, timeline.eisenhowermemorial.gov.
2  *New York Amsterdam News*, October 5, 1957.

# RESPONSES TO DESEGREGATION

**Reading Assignment**

*Chapters 9–12, pages 107–150 (abridged)*

## Overview

During Melba's first few weeks at Central High, she is spat on, kicked, threatened, and choked. Danny, the soldier who serves as her bodyguard, urges her to learn how to defend herself. He reminds her that he will not always be at her side.

Just before the Thanksgiving break, Danny and the 101st depart, leaving the Arkansas National Guard in charge. By December, the harassment is becoming more organized. Melba is also finding herself more and more isolated, not only at school but also at home. Because she now rarely sees even longtime friends, Melba looks forward to her birthday party. She is disappointed when only her boyfriend, Vince, attends. Her other friends are afraid to come to her house.

As Melba reflects on the ways she and the other eight African American students respond to the isolation as well as the daily heckling and harassment, she expresses particular concern for her friend Minnijean. Just before Christmas vacation, two boys constantly taunt Minnijean and hassle her in the cafeteria. She manages to ignore them for a time. Then, one day, she is unable to continue to disregard the harassment. She drops her lunch tray, spilling a bowl of chili on one of the boys. She is promptly suspended from school.

## Exploring the Text

Ask students for their questions or comments about what they have read in this section. Then use the following questions as journal or discussion prompts to guide students' exploration of the text.

### Consider why change at Central High was a slow, often painful process.

1. Study the entries from Melba's diary. What does her diary suggest about the way attitudes begin to change? How important are small gestures—a smile, a kind act—in that process?

2. Two confrontations are described in this section of the book. The first is a meeting with the superintendent of schools. The second is the roundtable discussion for Black and white students. Compare and contrast the two encounters. In

what respects are they similar? What differences seem most striking? Which one is more likely to widen perspectives? Shatter stereotypes?

### Trace the effects of Melba's experiences at Central High.

3. Ask a volunteer to read aloud the entry from Melba's diary on page 109 of the abridged version. What does it suggest about Melba's feelings about school? About the choices she has made?

4. Find at least two examples in the text of the way those feelings are beginning to change.

### Consider the effects of integration on Melba and the other African American students.

5. How does Melba's enrollment at Central High School affect her relationship with her old friends? Why do you think they are no longer willing to socialize with her?

6. How do Melba and the other eight African American students respond to the stresses at Central High?

7. How do NAACP officials want Melba and other students to respond to harassment? Why do you think they advise the students to avoid retaliating? How successful are Melba and the other students in following those instructions?

8. How do you explain Minnijean's response to the boys who taunt her? What is the short-term effect of her action? What do you think the long-term effect will be? Why do you think the school authorities respond as they do?

### Explore the meaning of the word *integration*.

9. What does Melba mean when she writes that "integration is a much bigger word than I thought" (page 113, abridged)?

10. Identify the various ways that the word *integration* is used in this reading. What does the word *integration* mean to Melba? To the other African American students at Central High? To white students there? How do you define the word?

### Consider how the author uses newspaper headlines and diary entries to underscore the importance of various events and experiences.

11. How do the quotations from the author's diary relate to the story the author tells?

12. Ask a volunteer to read aloud an incident or experience that includes a diary entry. Have a second volunteer read aloud the same passage without the diary entry. What does the entry add to our understanding?

13. How does the author use newspaper headlines? What do they add to our understanding of the events she describes?

14. How does the author use diary entries? What do they add to our understanding of the events she describes? How is the impact of the diary entries on the reader similar to or different from the impact of newspaper headlines?

# Connecting to the Central Question

After exploring the text and reviewing the events that take place in this section of the book, provide students with an opportunity to revisit their thinking about this guide's central question:

**Q:** *What can we do, alone and with others, to confront racism? How can we as individuals and as citizens make a positive difference in our school, community, and nation?*

Give students a few minutes to write down their thoughts in response to this question in light of what they have learned about the difficulties Melba and the other eight African American students faced at school during the fall of 1957. What does it take for these nine students to persist in the face of opposition from segregationists in their school and community? What do their experiences in this section of the book suggest about what is necessary to succeed in creating positive change in society?

# Activities for Deeper Understanding

### 1. Explore Teacher Engagement at Central High

Melba describes her teachers, with a few exceptions, as uninterested and unsympathetic. Was her impression accurate? Distribute the reading The Teachers at Central High and use the connection questions for a classroom discussion.

### 2. Little Rock Students Discuss Desegregation

In October 1957, just a month after school opened, NBC asked a number of Central High students to participate in a roundtable discussion moderated by Jorunn Ricketts, to be aired nationally. Melba Pattillo Beals describes it on pages 125 to 127 of the abridged edition. Invite seven students to read aloud from the transcript of the discussion, A Roundtable Discussion, and then, as a class, respond to the connection questions that follow the reading.

### 3. Journal Prompts

In addition to responding to the reading selection and continuing to add information to their timelines, suggest that students respond to the following writing prompts:

- Imagine that you had been asked to participate in the roundtable discussion. What questions would you have liked to ask? What would you have liked the other participants to know?

- Think of a time when you were insulted. Write about the experience, explaining what you decided to do and why you made that choice. Do you think you made the right choice?

# Extension Activity

## Investigate Other Student Voices

Invite students to research and report on the way other students at Central High, both Black and white, viewed the events Melba describes. Lesson 4 in Facing History's unit Choices in Little Rock (see facinghistory.org/warriors-media) includes documents that examine the events at Central High from the perspectives of a variety of students.

# The Teachers at Central High

Melba describes her teachers, with a few exceptions, as uninterested and unsympathetic. Daisy Bates, president of the Arkansas NAACP, viewed them from a different perspective. In her autobiography, she says of them:

> Many of the teachers—particularly the younger ones—did everything within their power to protect the nine students. Some went out of their way to help the students catch up with work they had missed when they were barred from entering the school in the first weeks of the term. Concerned over the lack of protection given the Negro students within the school, the teachers took it upon themselves to oversee the hallways in between the class breaks.[1]

At the end of the school year, when segregationists took over the school board, 44 teachers—many of whom taught at Central High—were fired for perceived support of integration.

## Connection Questions

1. How do Daisy Bates's observations and the firings complicate your view of the teachers at Central High? Why might Melba have had such a different impression of them?

2. How far do you think teachers' responsibilities should extend in protecting their students?

[1] Daisy Bates, *The Long Shadow of Little Rock: A Memoir* (Fayetteville: University of Arkansas Press, 1986), 144.

# A Roundtable Discussion

A month after school opened, NBC set up a roundtable discussion moderated by Jorunn Ricketts. The excerpt that follows focuses on comments made by four white students who participated in the discussion—Sammie Dean Parker, Kay Bacon, Robin Woods, and Joseph Fox—and two African American students, Ernest Green and Minnijean Brown.

**Ricketts:** Do you think it is possible to start working this out on a more sensible basis than violent demonstration?

**Sammie:** No. I don't because the South has always been against racial mixing and I think they will fight this thing to the end. . . . We fight for our freedom—that's one thing. And we don't have any freedom any more.

**Ernest:** Sammie, you say you don't have any freedom. I wonder what you mean by it—that you don't have any freedom? You are guaranteed your freedom in the Bill of Rights and your Constitution. You have the freedom of speech—I noticed that has been exercised a whole lot in Little Rock. The freedom of petition, the freedom of religion and the other freedoms are guaranteed to you. As far as freedom, I think that if anybody should kick about freedoms, it should be us. Because I think we have been given a pretty bad side on this thing as far as freedom.

**Sammie:** Do you call those troops freedom? I don't. And I also do not call it free when you are being escorted into the school every morning.

**Ernest:** Why did the troops come here? It is because our government—our state government—went against the federal law. . . . Our country is set up so that we have forty-eight states and no one state has the ability to overrule our nation's government. I thought that was what our country was built around. I mean, that is why we fight. We fought in World War II together—the fellows that I know died in World War II, they died in the Korean War. I mean, why should my friends get out there and die for a cause called "democracy" when I can't exercise my rights—tell me that. . . .

**Joe:** Well, Sammie, I don't know what freedom has been taken away from you because the truth is—I know as a senior myself—the troops haven't kept me from going to my classes or participating in any school activity. I mean, they're there just to keep order in case—I might use the term "hotheads"— get riled up. But I think as long as—if parents would just stay out of it and let the children of the school at Central High figure it out for themselves, I think it would be a whole lot better. I think the students are mature enough to figure it out for themselves. . . . As far as I'm concerned, I'll lay the whole blame of this trouble in Governor Faubus's lap.

**Sammie:** I think we knew before this ever started that some day we were going to have to integrate the schools. And I think our Governor was trying to protect all of us when he called out the National Guard—and he was trying to prepare us, I think.

**Ernest:** Well, I have to disagree. . . . I know a student that's over there with us, Elizabeth [Eckford], and that young lady, she walked two blocks, I guess—as you all know—and the mob was behind her. Did the troops break up the mob?

**Robin:** And when Elizabeth had to walk down in front of the school I was there and I saw that. And may I say, I was very ashamed—I felt like crying—because she was so brave when she did that. And we just weren't behaving ourselves—just jeering her. I think if we had had any sort of decency, we wouldn't have acted that way. But I think if everybody would just obey the Golden Rule—do unto others as you would have others do unto you—[it] might be the solution. How would you like to have to . . . walk down the street with everybody yelling behind you like they yelled behind Elizabeth?

**Ricketts:** Sammie, why do these children not want to go to school with Negroes?

**Sammie:** Well, I think it is mostly race mixing.

**Ricketts:** Race mixing? What do you mean?

**Sammie:** Well, marrying each other.

**Minnijean:** Hold your hand up. I'm brown, you are white. What's the difference? We are all of the same thoughts. You're thinking about your boy—he's going to the Navy. I'm thinking about mine—he's in the Air Force. We think about the same thing.

**Sammie:** I'll have to agree with you. . . .

**Minnijean:** Kay, Joe and Robin—do you know anything about me, or is it just what your mother has told you about Negroes?

**Ricketts:** Have you ever really made an effort to find out what they're like?

**Kay:** Not until today.

**Sammie:** Not until today.

**Ricketts:** And what do you think about it after today?

**Kay:** Well, you know that my parents and a lot of the other students and their parents think the Negroes aren't equal to us. But—I don't know. It seems like they are, to me.

**Sammie:** These people are—we'll have to admit that.

**Ernest:** I think, like we're doing today, discussing our different views. . . . If the people of Little Rock . . . would get together I believe they would find out a different story—and try to discuss the thing instead of getting out in the street and kicking people around and calling names—and that sort of thing. If . . . people got together it would be smoothed over.

**Kay:** I think that if . . . our friends had been getting in this discussion today, I think that maybe some of them—not all of them—in time, they would change their mind. But probably some of them would change their mind today.[1]

## Connection Questions

1. To what extent does the discussion help the students understand each other?

2. What does the discussion suggest about the role adults played in the events at Central High? How do you think the white students might have acted if the adults had been less involved?

1 "Transcript of Mrs. Jorunn Ricketts' Conversation," *New York Times*, October 14, 1957.

3. What fears do the white students articulate? What concerns do the African American students voice?

4. Suppose the school (instead of the media) had organized a series of informal discussions between Black and white students. Who might have benefited? What might students have learned from one another? When should these discussions have taken place?

# RESPONDING TO HARASSMENT

## Reading Assignment

*Chapters 13–16, pages 151–182 (abridged)*

## Overview

During Christmas vacation, Melba worries that Minnijean's suspension will give segregationists the issue they need to drive all nine African American students from Central High. Still, she enjoys the break from school and the family get-togethers, including a visit from her father. However, she remains isolated from old friends. She also feels increasingly distant from her boyfriend, Vince.

When school reopens, the harassment begins again. As Melba becomes more and more depressed, her grandmother advises her to respond to her tormentors with a smile or even a thank you. Melba also studies Mahatma Gandhi's teachings on nonviolence. Minnijean, who is readmitted with the understanding that she will not respond to harassment in any way, remains stoic even when soup is dumped on her. But when the attacks continue, she retaliates verbally and is expelled. The NAACP arranges for Minnijean to attend a private school in New York.

Melba continues to discipline herself to face each new school day. The one day she lets down her guard, she becomes the target of an attack. A white student named Link unexpectedly comes to her rescue, secretly warning her of an impending attack and lending her his car to make her escape. In the days that follow, Link joins those who heckle and threaten her at school. Yet at the same time, he warns her of future attacks. Although Melba's mother and grandmother doubt Link's motives, Melba comes to trust him.

## Exploring the Text

Ask students for their questions or comments about what they have read in this section. Then use the following questions as journal or discussion prompts to guide students' exploration of the text.

### Compare and contrast the strategies Melba develops in response to the growing harassment at school.

1. Identify the strategies Melba and the other students develop in response to harassment at school. What are the advantages of each? The drawbacks?

2. How does Melba's grandmother suggest that Melba disarm her attackers? How effective is that strategy?

3. In 1997, Elizabeth Eckford was asked why she returned to Central High after her experience with the mob. She replied, "Somewhere along the line, very soon [staying at Central] became an obligation. I realized that what we were doing was not for ourselves." What is that obligation? Is Melba's determination to remain at Central High the result of a similar feeling of obligation?

### Discuss the importance of community support to Melba and the other African American students at Central High.

4. How do some individuals and groups in the African American community show their support for Melba and the other eight students? What does that support mean to Melba?

5. Why are other individuals and groups in the African American community critical of the efforts of the nine students to integrate Central High? What does their lack of support mean to Melba?

### Consider what it means to take a stand against injustice at Central High School.

6. Why do you think Link secretly helps Melba elude her attackers?

7. What risks is Link taking in offering Melba his friendship? What risks is Melba taking in becoming friends with Link?

8. Why are Melba's mother and grandmother suspicious of Link's motives in befriending Melba?

9. Consider earlier incidents in the book when Melba has to keep a secret because of prejudice and discrimination. What does Melba's secret friendship with Link have in common with those incidents? What differences seem most striking?

10. Why does Link want Melba to tell the press that the situation at Central High School is improving? What does he hope the results of such a statement will be? How does she respond?

## Connecting to the Central Question

After exploring the text and reviewing the events that take place in this section of the book, provide students with an opportunity to revisit their thinking about this guide's central question:

**Q:** *What can we do, alone and with others, to confront racism? How can we as individuals and as citizens make a positive difference in our school, community, and nation?*

Give students a few minutes to write down their thoughts in response to this question in light of what they have learned about the difficulties Melba and the other eight African American students faced during the second half of the school year. How do the actions of new allies Melba meets in this section affect your thinking about what we can do to confront racism?

## Activities for Deeper Understanding

### 1. Walking a Tightrope

Ask students to read the poem I'll Walk the Tightrope and answer the questions that follow on a separate sheet of paper. Then have students use those answers to write a paragraph comparing Melba with the narrator in the poem. Have students share their answers with the class. Encourage students to think of a time when they too felt that they were "walking the tightrope." How did they keep their balance? Where did they find support?

### 2. Minnijean Brown in New York

Ask students whether they think Minnijean Brown was better off in New York. Then distribute the reading Minnijean Brown in New York and use the connection questions for class discussion.

### 3. Journal Prompt

In addition to responding to the reading selection and continuing to add information to their timelines, suggest that students respond to the following writing prompt:

What does it mean to have a friend? To be a friend? How do secrets affect friendships?

## Extension Activity

### Intergroup Contact Theory

Psychologist Gordon Allport studied prejudice and how to resist it. One of his most important ideas, known as intergroup contact theory, suggests that bringing people from different groups together can help reduce prejudice if certain conditions are met. Distribute the Intergroup Contact Theory reading and use the connection questions for classroom discussion.

# I'll Walk the Tightrope

Margaret Danner was an African American poet who grew up in the 1920s and 1930s. The following poem of hers is titled "I'll Walk the Tightrope."

> I'll walk the tightrope that's been stretched for me,
>
> and though a wrinkled forehead, perplexed why,
>
> will accompany me, I'll delicately
>
> step along. For if I stop to sigh
>
> at the earth-propped stride
>
> of others, I will fall. I must balance high
>
> without a parasol to tide
>
> a faltering step, without a net below,
>
> without a balance stick to guide.[1]

## Connection Questions

1. What do you think it is like to "balance high" without a parasol, net, or balance stick? How does the person on a tightrope keep from falling?

2. How are Melba and the other eight African American students at Central High like the narrator in the poem? What keeps them from falling?

3. Have you ever "walked the tightrope"? What kept you from falling? How did you keep your balance?

1    Margaret Danner, "I'll Walk the Tightrope," *Poem: Counterpoem* (Detroit: Broadside Press, 1969).

# Minnijean Brown in New York

After Minnijean Brown was expelled from Central High, the NAACP arranged for her to go to school in New York. The editors of the *New York Post* welcomed Minnijean to New York with these words:

> When a Negro girl is so drastically penalized for reacting as a human being under fire, it is no wonder that white youngsters in the school feel safe to resume the business of bullying. . . .

> Minnijean will find the [racial] demarcation line here less obvious. But part of the education she gets in Our Town will be the knowledge that we too practice racial discrimination, though more subtly than the folks back home. We hope it doesn't come as too much of a shock to her to discover the difference between New York and Little Rock is not as great as it should be. Possibly her arrival will inspire us to be worthy of her and the cause for which she and other Southern Negro children have stood so stoically and so valiantly. Little Rock's loss is our proud acquisition.[1]

## Connection Questions

1. What are the editors suggesting about the similarities between New York and Little Rock? About the differences between the two cities?

1  *New York Post* editorial (February 19, 1958), quoted in Daisy Bates, *The Long Shadow of Little Rock: A Memoir* (Fayetteville: University of Arkansas Press, 1986), 121.

# Intergroup Contact Theory

In criminology, psychology, and sociology, the contact hypothesis has been described as one of the best ways to improve relations among groups that are experiencing conflict. Gordon W. Allport is often credited with the development of the contact hypothesis, also known as intergroup contact theory. The premise of Allport's theory states that under appropriate conditions, interpersonal contact is one of the most effective ways to reduce prejudice between majority and minority group members.

If one has the opportunity to communicate with others, one is able to understand and appreciate different points of view. As a result of new appreciation and understanding, prejudice should diminish. Issues of stereotyping, prejudice, and discrimination are commonly occurring issues between rival groups. Allport's proposal was that properly managed contact between such groups should reduce these problems and lead to better interactions.

Contact fails to cure conflict when contact situations create anxiety for those who take part. Contact situations need to be long enough to allow this anxiety to decrease and for the members of the conflicting groups to feel comfortable with one another. Additionally, if the members of the two groups use this contact situation to trade insults, argue with each other, resort to physical violence, and discriminate against each other, contact should not be expected to reduce conflict between groups. To obtain beneficial effects, the situation must include positive contact. Some of the criteria are as follows:

1. **Equal status.** Both groups must engage equally in the relationship. Members of the group should have similar backgrounds, qualities, and characteristics. Differences in academic backgrounds, wealth, skill, or experiences should be minimized if these qualities will influence perceptions of prestige and rank in the group.

2. **Common goals.** Both groups must work on a problem/task and share this as a common goal, sometimes called a superordinate goal—a goal that can only be attained if the members of two or more groups work together by pooling their efforts and resources.

3. **Intergroup cooperation.** Both groups must work together toward their common goals without competition.

4. **Support of authorities, law, or customs.** Both groups must acknowledge some authority that supports the contact and interactions between the groups. The contact should encourage friendly, helpful, egalitarian attitudes and condemn ingroup–outgroup comparisons.

5. **Personal interaction.** The contact situation needs to involve informal, personal interaction with outgroup members. Members of the conflicting groups need to mingle with one another. Without this criterion, they learn very little about each other, and cross-group friendships do not occur.[1]

---

1 "Contact Hypothesis," Wikipedia, https://en.wikipedia.org/wiki/Contact_hypothesis, accessed June 9, 2014.

## Connection Questions

1. Intergroup contact theory states that under appropriate conditions, interpersonal contact is one of the most effective ways to reduce prejudice between majority and minority group members. Which of these five conditions was met during the desegregation efforts in Little Rock? Which issues may have presented challenges to meeting those conditions?

2. Can you think of current examples—in your school, the community, the country, or internationally—that support or refute Allport's theory?

# LEGACIES

## Reading Assignment

*Pages 183–226 (abridged)*

## Overview

Melba continues her friendship with Link despite her family's concerns about his motives. At his urgent request, she goes with him to see his former nanny, an elderly African American woman. Melba not only helps Link find a doctor for the ailing woman but also persuades her grandmother to help care for her.

As the school year draws to a close, segregationists step up their efforts to force the remaining African Americans from the school. This time they focus on the students' families. Melba's mother is told that her teaching contract will not be renewed unless Melba withdraws from Central High. She keeps her job only after an African American bishop in her church intervenes on her behalf.

Throughout that spring, Ernest Green, the only senior among the African American students, is the focus of much of the harassment. The segregationists want to keep him from graduating. Although they fail, the only African Americans allowed to attend the ceremony are members of Ernest's family. Melba listens to the graduation on the radio.

Link, distraught over the death of Mrs. Healy, asks Melba to accompany him to school in the North. Melba refuses, telling him she is going to remain at Central High. But she never gets the opportunity. Despite a Supreme Court ruling that integration must continue, Governor Faubus closes all of the high schools in Little Rock in the fall of 1958. To continue her education, Melba goes to live with a white family in California. With the support of her adopted family, she finishes high school there and goes on to college.

## Exploring the Text

Ask students for their questions or comments about what they have read in this section. Then use the following questions as journal or discussion prompts to guide students' exploration of the text.

### Consider the effects of racism on the choices Link makes.

1. Why does Link feel responsible for Mrs. Healy? Why do you think his parents do not feel as responsible for her welfare?

2. How does Link's relationship with Mrs. Healy affect his attitude toward African Americans?

3. How does racism affect Link's friendship with Melba?

4. To what extent does Link take a stand against racism?

### Discuss the importance of Ernest Green's graduation.

5. What does Ernest Green's graduation from Central High School mean to African Americans in Little Rock? Why is it a matter of such concern to segregationists?

6. School officials tell the Greens that only members of their family can attend the graduation, but the family secretly arranges for two outsiders to attend: one is a reporter for a Black newspaper, and the other is Dr. Martin Luther King Jr. Why do you think the family invites these two strangers to the graduation? Why do you think both choose to attend? What does their presence suggest about the effect the nine students have had on African Americans throughout the nation?

### Consider the consequences of the choices Melba and the other eight African American students make.

7. What have Melba and the other African American students accomplished? To what extent have they made a difference in Little Rock? In cities across the nation? To people around the world?

8. What groups honor Melba and the other African American students? Besides giving recognition to the students, what message are the groups conveying to other Americans?

9. Why is Melba so committed to returning to the school in September?

### Consider why Melba regards her experiences at Central High as a positive force in her life.

10. Melba writes that "the newspapers said Ernie's diploma cost the taxpayers half a million dollars. Of course, we knew it cost all of us much more." What does she mean?

11. Why do you think Melba comes to see her Central High experience as "a positive force that has shaped the course of my life"? How has it shaped her identity?

12. What experiences have been a positive force in your life? How have they shaped your identity?

## Connecting to the Central Question

After exploring the text and reviewing the events that take place in this section of the book, provide students with an opportunity to revisit their thinking about this guide's central question:

**Q:** *What can we do, alone and with others, to confront racism? How can we as individuals and as citizens make a positive difference in our school, community, and nation?*

Give students a few minutes to write down their thoughts in response to this question in light of what they have learned about what happened as the school year came to an end. Was the 1957–1958 school year a success for the Little Rock Nine? What do the events at the end of the school year and afterward suggest about the process of overcoming racism?

# Activities for Deeper Understanding

## 1. The Enduring Legacy of Little Rock

The crisis in Little Rock didn't end with the last day of school. Distribute the reading The Continuing Crisis in Little Rock and use the connection questions as journal prompts or class discussion.

## 2. Reader Response

The Reader Response handout provides students with an opportunity to summarize their understanding of the book. The questions encourage critical thinking about the story and personal responses to its themes. After students have completed their answers to the questions, you may want to focus a class discussion on their responses.

## 3. The Lesson to Be Learned

In 1996, seven of the African American students who attended Central High during the 1957–1958 school year appeared on *The Oprah Winfrey Show*. They came face to face with a few of the white students who tormented them as well as one student who befriended them. In reflecting on the year, a white student said, "I didn't understand why you all wanted to come to Central High School, why you would want to leave your friends, things that you knew and were comfortable with, and why you would even want to be with me."

Ask students how they would respond to the man's comments. Did the African American students put up with harassment just to be with white students? Why did they risk their lives? How important was the stand they took? Ernest Green told the audience that "if there's any lesson to be learned," it is to "stand up for what's right."

Have students review the writing and discussion they have done in response to *Warriors Don't Cry*. What injustices upset them most? How might they and their friends confront these injustices? This discussion may be used to introduce the assessment at the end of this guide.

# The Continuing Crisis in Little Rock

The Rev. Colbert Cartwright was one of the few white ministers in Little Rock to speak out against the mob. He and other religious leaders organized a day of prayer for peace in the city on October 12, 1957. Although over 6,000 people participated, the next day the crowds gathered once again outside Central High. And once again, white citizens closed their doors to the violence or chose to look the other way. In reflecting on what he learned from the crisis in Little Rock, Cartwright observed:

> In the end, the law could not do it [integrate the schools]. A group of very dedicated people, women . . . marshaled . . . grassroots support to take back the schools and work on the desegregation problem. The lesson is that people themselves had to take responsibility for what they wanted their community to be. . . . They had to rally the good forces in the community to take back the schools, do more than a lackluster desegregation effort by some edict. This was work that should have been done prior to desegregation.[1]

Sara Alderman Murphy was one of the women who worked to reopen the city's schools after they were closed for the 1958–1959 school year. Her experience convinced her that "Little Rock was split into two communities that did not communicate or know enough about each other to solve problems together." She decided that "work needed to be done in changing attitudes—my own as well as others."[2] In 1963, she organized the Panel of American Women. It was an interfaith, interracial group that provided speakers for civic clubs, religious groups, and women's organizations in Little Rock and beyond.

One evening, Mildred Terry, a member of the panel, spoke to a group about her son Alvin. He was one of the first Black students at a local junior high school. She described how he was punched in the back, knocked down stairs, and repeatedly called names by white students at the school. After the program, a white boy about the same age as her son asked to speak privately with her. She later shared that conversation with Murphy. Murphy recalled:

> When he and Terry were alone, he said, "You don't know me but you would if I told you my name. I was one of those boys who harassed Alvin. I hadn't thought about how it made him feel until I heard you talking today. Please tell him I'm sorry I did it." "I certainly did remember his name when he gave it," Terry said later, laughing. "He made Alvin's life miserable but I can't get over what he said today. I was really moved to know he finally understood what he had done."[3]

## The End of the Story?

Although the high schools in Little Rock reopened in the fall of 1959, the process of desegregating Central High and other schools across the country unfolded slowly. Additional civil rights laws, such as the 1964 Civil Rights Act, and new court orders demanding that schools comply with *Brown v. Board of Education* helped the process. But when faced with sending their children to desegregated schools, many white

---

1   Interview with Colbert Cartwright by Mimi Dortch, 1993 Arkansas Interfaith Conference, quoted in Sara Alderman Murphy, *Breaking the Silence: Little Rock's Women's Emergency Committee to Open Our Schools, 1958–1963* (Fayetteville: University of Arkansas Press, 1997), 58.
2   Alderman Murphy, *Breaking the Silence*, 244.
3   Alderman Murphy, *Breaking the Silence*, 246.

families in Little Rock and across the South chose to send their children to the increasing number of private schools instead. Yet persistent efforts at school desegregation did bring about change at Central High. Historian Hasan Kwame Jeffries writes:

> In recent years, Little Rock Central's student population has been 58 percent black, 30 percent white, 8 percent Asian and 4 percent Hispanic; the school has also been among Arkansas' best performing in terms of graduation rates and achievement on standardized tests. "This is my school," said black student Malik Marshall a few years back when he was enrolled there. "I love it here."[4]

At Central High School, the honors classes are mainly white. The regular classes are primarily African American. No one seems sure why this is so. Some think it is due to racism. Others attribute it to the poor academic preparation of incoming Black students. Jeffries continues:

> [T]hings have been far from perfect at Central. "We're desegregated," said Marshall, referring to the fact that racial divisions were plain to see inside the school. "We're not integrated because integration comes from the heart of the people that go here. . . . It's something that you have to want to do," he added.

> Desegregation, though, is the necessary starting point for integration, and few schools have made this long, arduous journey as successfully. The question, then, is why is Central High such an anomaly?[5]

According to the Civil Rights Project at UCLA, despite the absence of segregation laws, school segregation has risen significantly since the early 1990s everywhere in the United States, in both the North and the South. A third of African American and Latino students attend schools that have few or no white students. Jeffries writes that this trend demonstrates that "fully desegregating the nation's public schools will be neither quick nor easy." But the story of Central High School demonstrates that it is possible.[6]

## Connection Questions

1. What does the account of Central High School today suggest about the progress that has been made since 1958? What does it suggest about the work that remains?

2. How does Malik Marshall distinguish between the terms *desegregation* and *integration*? What does the information in this reading suggest is required to accomplish each?

3. What might be the consequences for students and communities of the trend toward school segregation since the 1990s? How has reading *Warriors Don't Cry* and learning about the struggle to desegregate Central High helped you understand these consequences?

4. What does Melba Pattillo Beals's story and the history of Central High suggest about the way communities can crack the walls that divide people? About the way we as individuals can make a positive difference?

4  Hasan Kwame Jeffries, "Little Rock 60 Years Later," *Teaching Tolerance* magazine (Southern Poverty Law Center project), Issue 57 (Fall 2017), accessed September 20, 2017, https://www.tolerance.org/magazine/fall-2017/little-rock-60-years-later.
5  Ibid.
6  Ibid.

# Reader Response

Write your answers to the following questions here or on a separate sheet of paper.

1. *Warriors Don't Cry* focuses on a single year in Melba Pattillo's life. Identify some of the internal and external conflicts she faced that year.

2. Describe how Melba's year at Central High has affected the way she sees herself and others.

3. How does Melba change in the course of the book? To what experiences does she attribute those changes? To what experiences do you attribute those changes?

4. What does Melba's story mean to you?

5. Why do you think she wrote this book?

6. What is the meaning of the title *Warriors Don't Cry*?

## Assessment

# RESPONDING TO THE CENTRAL QUESTION

Throughout their study of *Warriors Don't Cry*, students have been developing their thinking about a central question concerning what we can do to confront racism. Before concluding your study of the memoir, consider having students respond to the central question in a formal assignment or activity in order to demonstrate what they have learned.

We recommend having students respond to the central question in an essay assignment. A structured class discussion, such as a Socratic Seminar, may help students further develop their thinking before writing their essays (or you might use such a discussion instead of the essay).

You can use the following prompt to guide students' responses to the central question, regardless of the format you choose for the activity:

**Q:** *What can we do, alone and with others, to confront racism? How can we as individuals and as citizens make a positive difference in our school, community, and nation? Use examples from* Warriors Don't Cry *and other resources you have explored while studying the book to support your thinking.*

Facing History's Writing Strategies guide (see facinghistory.org/warriors-media) provides a variety of activities and strategies to help you guide students in completing the writing process and publishing their essays. We recommend that you consult this resource as students

- craft a thesis and organize their ideas;

- support the thesis with evidence and analysis;

- write an introduction and conclusion;

- draft, revise, and edit their essays; and

- publish and share their essays and reflect on the writing process.

# Credits

"Merry-Go-Round" by Langston Hughes, from *The Collected Poems of Langston Hughes*. Copyright © 1994 by the Estate of Langston Hughes. Reproduced by permission from Penguin Random House and Georges Borchardt.